Treasures of the Heart
Prose and Poetry Refreshing the Soul
Developing a Deeper Walk with God

Biblical Devotional Poetry

By Kenneth L. Birks

~

Published by
Straight Arrow Publications

Second Edition

www.straitarrow.net

Copyright 2023

Cover and Interior Design by Ken Birks

Cover Formatted by Hans Bennewitz
design / illustration / art direction
hans@modedesign.us
www.hansbennewitz.com

Unless otherwise indicated, all Scripture quotations are taken from The Holy Bible, New King James Version @ 1982 by Thomas Nelson, Included

*Chosen by God as peculiar treasures, in Him, we delight.
Distributing gifts to all, He pours into our vessels to
ignite. Given for the profit of all, His body, He desires
to glorify. Given to aid in ministry, we press to receive
His best. As flames of fire burning with passion,
we press to bless.*

*But we have this treasure in earthen vessels, that the
excellency of the power may be of God and not of us.*

2 Corinthians 4:7

Foreword

As you read through the devotional prose and poetry found in this book, you will find a beautiful blend of timeless truths fitly applied to today's culture and challenges that fill your heart with treasures from above. The Heavenly insights will challenge you to grow in the knowledge of the Son of God, enabling you to excel in all that God is calling you to be and do.

Each devotional poem stands on its own, but together, they will propel you into a rewarding journey of experiencing the treasures God desires to fill your heart with as you journey through this life. This book's prose and poetry writings are intended to call you away from all that distracts so that your heart can be set on what brings delight to your soul and our Heavenly Father above.

As one reviewer said, *"The majestic flow from one poem to the next contains powerful prophetic wisdom and revelation that will fill your hearts and minds with the wonderful treasures God intends you to enjoy. The prose and poetry written here are very Davidic and musical, flowing like delightful streams of thought with heavenly impartations as you receive encouragement to fulfill all our Heavenly Father has commissioned you to be and do."*

May God bless you richly as you meditate on the Word of God that has been interpreted into Holy impartations of encouragement and blessings through prose and poetry.

Treasures of the Heart
Prose and Poetry Refreshing the Soul
Developing a Deeper Walk with God

By Kenneth L. Birks

Table of Contents

Peculiar Treasures	1	Hearts Aflame	29
Heart Treasures Unlocked	2	Intimately Acquainted	30
Holy Spirit Rejuvenation	3	Pressing on in Faith	32
Manifesting Christ's Presence	4	Multiplying What's Sown	33
Cultivating Your Heart	5	Shifting Paradigms	34
Joyful Treasures of the Heart	6	Voice of the Sentry	35
Kairos Moments of the Heart	7	Peace Amid Turbulence	37
Empowered by His Presence	8	Avoiding Foolish Chatter	38
Looking Out My Window	9	In You Alone	39
The Goodness of God	10	Perfect in Righteousness	40
Triumphant Living Gained	11	Embracing God's Peace	41
Drawn to the Light	12	Quickened by His Word	42
Quickened for Spiritual Labor	13	Breaking Free to Run	43
Captivated by His Love	14	Hearts Freely Committed	45
The Heart's Portals	15	Awakened by the Sunrise	46
Bloom Where You're Planted	16	Looking to God in All	47
Innumerable Treasures	17	Lights Amid Darkness	49
From Despondency to Hope	18	Breaking Through	50
Love Comes to All	19	Kingdom Powered Life	51
Fruit of the Spirit Treasured	20	Faith Erupts	52
Unfailing Love of the Father	21	As the Wheel Turns	53
Treasures of Love and Mercy	22	Homeward Bound	54
Holy Spirit, Our Helper	23	Ken's Poetic Testimony	56
Strength and Courage	24		
Treasured Stones Found	25	About the Author	58
Delighting in His Presence	26	Books & Workbooks	59
From Heaven Above	27	Reviews and References	63
Waiting on the Lord	28	Online Connections	65

Peculiar Treasures

Chosen by God, peculiar treasures we become.
In His delight, our hearts align, forever one.
Pouring gifts into our vessels, flames ignite.
For His body to profit, we proclaim His might.

Like flames of fire, we press forward with zeal.
Harvest fields of blessing, many quickly heal.
Prophecies revealing divulge core conditions.
Faith's challenges met, divine nature positions.

Gifts of healing and miracles, our hands extend.
Crowds gather, drawn by wonders that transcend.
Discerning spirits dismantle darkness' hold,
Demonic strongholds crumbling, truth unfolds.

Knit together as lively stones, we find our place.
Each gift strategically positioned in God's grace,
Freely given, freely explored, His glory we embrace.
Bathed in His radiance, multitudes seek His face.

The sickle put to the harvest, the earth reaped,
A greater harvest awaits, fully developed, steeped,
As one body, fully equipped, we rise in formation,
To every tribe and nation, we carry His salvation.

Armed with spiritual weapons, Satan stands aghast.
His schemes unraveling, the anointed move fast.
The Day of the Lord approaching, eternity appeals.
The millennial period, reigning, triumph reveals.

~

In whom the whole building, being fitted together, grows into a holy temple in the Lord, in whom you also are being built together for a dwelling place in the Spirit.
Ephesians 2:21-22

Treasures of the Heart Unlocked

Hidden in obscurity, desires unachieved lie in wait.
Areas of the heart remaining locked, destiny lingers.
Hidden in the recesses of the heart, treasures await.
In obscurity, that which begs to be opened, unlocks.
Eyes of understanding enlightened, discovery inflates.

Holding the keys, insight reveals the kingdom within.
Questions seizing, light breaks through cracks therein.
Insight giving way, hearts once locked give way to light.
Treasures glimpsed; hope appears for what's exposed.
Undetected areas revealed; treasures appear disclosed.

Destiny no longer lingering, divine abilities unearth.
Faith moving forward, all things about life disperse.
Treasures opened; the heart presses on in fervency.
Forgetting the past, it reaches laying hold fearlessly.
Freed from darkness, the heart rejoices in discovery.

Seasons changing, treasures appear as required.
With change, new treasures wait to be opened.
Holding the keys, He gives freely as needed or desired.
Unlocking innate and divine, new treasures appear.
Oh, to know Him, who has the keys to the kingdom.

∼

That the God of our Lord Jesus Christ, the Father of glory, may give to you the Spirit of wisdom and revelation in the knowledge of Him the eyes of your understanding being enlightened; that you may know what the hope of His calling is, what are the riches of the glory of His inheritance in the saints.
Ephesians 1:17-18

Rejuvenated by the Holy Spirit

Self-centered ways demoralizing, we look for comfort.
Same results wearing down, we look for something new.
Magic formulas dooming, we dismantle to pursue.
Embittered and stuck in past ideologies, we collide.
Dreams no longer empowering, disillusionment decides.

Empowerment from above, piqued, we give ear.
Interest rekindled; we embrace newness without fear.
Hope materialized; we consider what's left behind.
In childlike faith, we embrace foreign thinking.
Nothing to lose; we consider new ways, trusting.

From faith to faith, unknown paths become clear.
Given to the path wholeheartedly, we commit.
Fully realized, we give ourselves to the Holy Spirit.
Self-sufficiency destroyed; His sufficiency sustains.
Empowered by His Spirit, we press on in all given.

His Holy Spirit released; heated passion stirs within.
Faith and belief merging, His Spirit produces therein.
Fresh vision empowering, we press forward to gain.
Confusion crucified; His Spirit frees to obtain.
Obedience embraced; we celebrate victory to retain.

~

However, when He, the Spirit of truth, has come, He will guide you into all truth; for He will not speak on His own authority, but whatever He hears, He will speak; and He will tell you things to come.
John 14:13

Manifesting Christ's Presence

Fruitful harvests in mind, the divine seed He plants.
Deep in the earth's crust, it bursts forth in His likeness.
As grains of wheat with many seeds, His seed multiplies.
Bursting forth in His likeness, the seed gives birth
In powerful displays of power, transformation emerges.

Growing rapidly, His planting springs forth, bearing leaves.
Born of the Spirit, passionate hearts produce in mass.
Watered by God's word, His plants multiply rapidly.
Emerging in abundance, fruit bursts forth in His likeness.
Spiritual growth evidenced, Christ's presence manifests.

Making no provision for the flesh, new nature emerges.
As newness in Christ emerges, the old disintegrates.
From glory to glory, He reveals Himself in those emerging.
Putting on new garments, the old are tossed aside.
Adding to their faith, virtue and self-control are applied.

Godliness, kindness, and love secured; newness completes.
In power and authority, uniqueness in fullness releases.
Knitted and joined together in likeness, His body emerges.
Fully surrendered, embracing His cross, His body magnifies.
Seed multiplied; Christ appears in glory through His body.

~

But we all, with unveiled face, beholding as in a mirror the glory of the Lord, are being transformed into the same image from glory to glory, just as by the Spirit of the Lord.
2 Corinthians 3:18

Cultivating Your Heart

Trampled by carnality and worldliness, the heart disengages.
Weighed down by worldly cares, the soil cries for righteousness.
Disillusionment taken over; the heart gives way to confusion.
Cracked and broken, the ground's soil yearns to be plowed.
With the promise of righteous rain, prayers for rain are heard.

Committed to cultivating fallow ground, repentance is pursued.
Coming as the early rain, His righteousness rains uninhibited.
Righteousness beginning to rain, His love softens the ground.
Cracks disappearing, righteousness covering, chains unbind.
Ground saturated, treasured hearts emerge renewed.

Newness emerging, transformation sprouts in refreshed reality.
Ground watered and nurtured; increase gives way to vitality.
With a spirit of joyfulness, the ground gives way to new fruit.
Immersed in wisdom and revelation, a surge of power is felt.
As downpours of righteousness extend, new fields are plowed.

Coming as the latter rain, covering the earth, He extends mercy.
Made entirely new, cultivated by His Spirit, the anointed rise.
In His fullness, fully matured, the harvest is beautiful and glorious.
The harvest completed, the earth's fruit is excellent and appealing.
Having escaped from worldliness, all stand ready for His return.

~

Sow for yourselves righteousness; reap in mercy; break up your fallow ground, for it is time to seek the Lord till He comes and rains righteousness on you.
Hosea 10:12

Joyful Treasures of the Heart

Awakened by thoughts swirling about, we listen joyfully.
With anticipation, we give of ourselves to Him faithfully.
In wonderment we stand amazed as joy penetrates.
Drawn to Him in intense joy that floods, we discover.
Embraced fully, joy reverberates with cleansing power.

Sin washed; guilt and shame disappear into the night.
Captivated by joyful treasures, in His benefits, we delight.
Tender mercies taking hold, angels rejoice over us.
No longer bound by sin, we delight in salvation.
Redeemed from destruction, our joyful hearts beat on.

Knowing joyfulness strengthens; Satan comes to steal.
With traps and snares, he comes to deceive and beguile.
Not ignorant of his devices, we stand ready to defend.
Hurling his darts, taking the shield of faith, we contend.
Filled with joy and a new countenance, we give praise.

From the wells of salvation, we draw while joy fills.
In the Spirit of wisdom and revelation, His joy fulfills.
Called according to His purposes, with joy, we lead.
Immersed in His Spirit with wisdom, revelation accedes.
In anticipation of heart treasures to come, joy exceeds.

∼

*Behold, God is my salvation, I will trust and not be afraid;
for Y*AH*, the* L*ORD, is my strength and song; He also has
become my salvation. Therefore, with joy, you will draw
water from the wells of salvation.*
Isaiah 12:2-3

Kairos Moments of the Heart

Awakened by His voice within, we rise in anticipation.
Gliding through landscapes of our minds, we look back.
Seeing His hand in all that's gone before us, we glimpse.
With deposits of faith, He gently caresses the heart.
Breathing in new life, the way forward is discovered.

His hand steadily upon us, insight propels forward.
Looking back with faith, His gentle leading is sensed.
Gazing steadily upon Him, destiny awakens within.
From faith to faith, His hand sensed; we rest in Him.
Brimming in confidence, pressing on, destiny awaits.

Fully awake, we rise in anticipation for what's next.
Power and might surging, He equips for the moment.
Giving ourselves to the moment, Kairos surprises.
Revelation and insight filling, instructions are given.
Grace empowering, tasks ahead are done with ease.

In awe of the moment, we envision with His purpose.
Filled with insight and vision, we stand ready for service.
Knowing life is full of Kairos moments, we rejoice in Him.
Faith rising from treasures, He completes what's begun.
In trust and assurance, we know destiny belongs to Him.

∼

Being confident of this very thing, that He who has begun a good work in you will complete it until the day of Jesus Christ.
Philippians 1:6

Empowered by His Presence

Empowered by His presence, we see clearly.
Embracing the cross, we discard ungodliness.
Knowing He's in charge, we die daily to self.
As He leads, we discover His abundance.
The path ahead lit, we no longer stumble.

With joy, we give praise for treasures given.
As peace takes hold, pain and sorrow leave.
His love washing over, we rejoice in Him.
No longer bound, we leave chains behind.
With freedom tasted, we run to attain.

Empowered to run, we reach for the prize.
Taking up residence, His kingdom reigns.
Shown things to come, we press forward.
With all things to gain, nothing holds back.
With the prize before us, we keep going.

Empowered by His presence, we taste His fruit.
Fruitfulness spreading, His fragrance releases.
As others taste, His presence spreads rapidly.
With treasures given, He becomes known to all.
Going forth, He empowers to all that's required.

Brethren, I do not count myself to have apprehended;
but one thing I do, forgetting those things which are behind and
reaching forward to those things which are ahead. I press toward
the goal for the prize of the upward call of God in Christ Jesus.
Philippians 3:13-14

Looking Out My Window

Looking out my window, I see God's wonders in the skies.
With expectations of a new day, sunrise is seen as it rises.
As the sun rises, eyes are blinded by its brightness above.
Gazing upon its beauty, revelation awakens with His love.

Looking out my window, I feel the sun's warmth so bright.
Squirrels play joyfully without thought or care of fright.
In the beauty of His created ones, God's hand is seen.
More than those who chirp and play, He delights in us.

Looking out my window, sadness is seen on some passing by.
As the homeless walk by, I wonder where they sleep tonight.
As the sun fades, it gives way to darkness with cold and bite.
I pray the provider supplies what's needed as the sun fades.

Looking out my window, mothers stroll joyfully by.
Rejoicing in their miracles of birth, they sing lullaby.
Gazing upon their beauty, their hearts fill with wonder.
Taking note of beauty and wonder of God, I give praise.

Looking out my window, stray cats bask in the sunlight.
The neighborhood their home, they disappear into the night.
Giving thanks, I give praise for the significance of a stray cat.
In awareness, I realize I'm more significant in His sight.

Looking out my window, all seen, I fill with amazement.
Seeing His handiwork, I rejoice in what's made for enjoyment.
Looking with care over what's conceived, peace liberates.
Wrapped in His tender love of care, the moment is enjoyed.

∼

Look at the birds of the air, for they neither sow nor reap nor gather into barns; yet your heavenly Father feeds them. Are you not of more value than they?
Matthew 6:26

The Goodness of God

Free to all, the goodness of God springs forth from love.
Those responding experience newness from above.
Freed from guilt, shame, and self-hatred; hearts fill with love.
With goodness received, insight and revelation flow freely.
Hearts wide open, freed from terrors, hearts flow fearlessly.

With the Father's goodness imparted, refreshing pours forth.
Repentance taking root, dryness of the soul refreshes.
As a mighty rushing river, the soul cleanses with forgiveness.
Giving way, streams of living water pour forth in abundance.
Beauty from newness within produces hearts of peace.

Like a guardrail, the goodness of God gives security.
A stronghold in days of trouble; anxiety disappears.
New strongholds in place, peace holds firm in disparity.
Through storms, waves of peace wash away all agitation.
As hope fills, its anchor holds steady as storms rage on.

Goodness taking root; body, soul, and spirit experience healing.
Where sickness and disease exist, now faith and healing for all.
Healing taking root; sin, and wounds give way to regeneration.
Where destruction was, now comes restoration from the fall.
Oh, that God's people would give thanks for His goodness to all.

~

The Lord is good, a stronghold in the day of trouble;
and He knows those who trust in Him.
Nahum 1:7

Triumphant Living Gained

Spurning piety for soulish desires, we resist deflation.
Misaligned, given to uselessness; we seek resolution.
Overwhelmed with circumstances, despair dejects.
Destructive ways, stuck in mire, hopelessness injects.
Reaping what's sown, we contemplate defection.

Reason returning; thoughts give way to stark realization.
Seeking relief from oppression, thoughts turn above.
No longer wise in our ways, we seek above for answers.
Promises of life filled with His abundance, we consider.
Light touching wounds inflicted; hope inflates.

A voice beckoning, we give ear to Him, who relieves.
Offering sufficiency in all, the way forward is shown.
Giving ear to His voice, He reveals the Son of God.
Faith in Him who shows the way, the past is forgiven.
Leaving all behind, we heartedly embrace His ways.

Embracing new life found, speaking softly, we listen.
Acknowledging Him in all ways, He directs our paths.
Taking the lead, wisdom and abundance fill the void.
No longer misaligned, He leads to triumphant ways.
Conquering spirits given; in Him, we rise to slay.

~

Now, thanks be to God, who always leads us in triumph in Christ and through us diffuses the fragrance of His knowledge in every place. For we are to God the fragrance of Christ among those who are being saved and among those who are perishing.
2 Corinthians 2:14-15

Drawn to the Light

Drawn to the light piercing the soul, we turn.
What revelation does this brilliance now discern?
With radiant glow, it tugs upon our core,
An oft-ignored path revealed, inviting more.

Stepping into the unknown, we fully embrace.
Newfound peace flooding replaces fear's trace.
Courage unrolling, faith's wings begin to soar.
Delight propelling forward, like lions, we roar.

Enlightenment swelling, the path's fruit emerges.
Invincibility erupting, newfound courage surges.
Freedom tasted, we follow the light, awestruck,
Led toward its source—the Son, whom we trust.

Investigating further, a gate found is sealed,
Holding the key, He whispers, "Trust and yield."
Confession spilling forth; hearts rejoice and sing.
Love's warmth washing over, surrender brings.

Keys to the kingdom, bestowed upon our quest,
Unlocking trials, treasures, gifts—divine bequest.
Faith to faith, righteousness blooms and thrives,
Mysteries revealed, destiny unfolds our lives.

No longer apprehensive, we tread paths revealed.
Darkness retreating, light's dominion is unsealed.
Dawn's glow upon us, we journey as He aligns,
The righteous way illuminated; purpose intertwines.

~

The path of the righteous is like the first gleam of dawn, which shines ever brighter until the full light of day.
Proverbs 4:18 NLT

Quickened for Spiritual Labor

Alarmed by all seen and heard, we stand in wonder.
Dark clouds hovering over, wickedness reigns.
Shaking off slumber once gripping, we rise in wonder.
Reminded; harvest is ripe, we seek Him above to fill.

Quickened, we present ourselves as His laborers.
Repentance filling our hearts, we turn in humility.
Repentance quickening, we break fallow ground.
Embracing the cross, we lose ourselves in Him.

Growth materializing: urgency stirs to action.
Harvest fields plentiful, we find places to sow.
Filled with faith, we prudently sow in expectation.
No longer self-absorbed, we diligently sow.

Dimensions of grace added, He equips for harvest.
Righteousness taking hold, He readies for gleaning.
Laborers quickened by His Spirit; He sends rain.
Rain falling hard, His harvest comes to full maturity.

Fully Immersed, His laborers go mightily, harvesting.
His anointed ones rising, He draws many to their light.
Darkness dissipating, they stand as a strong tower.
Will you be one who breaks up your fallow ground?

~

*Sow for yourselves righteousness; reap in mercy;
break up your fallow ground, for it is time to seek the LORD.*
Hosea 10:12

Captivated by His Love

Captivated by Your Love, we embrace You joyously.
Mercy washing over, You cleanse through and through.
Your enduring love captivating, we seek your nearness.
Thoughts captivated by love; we cling to Your presence.
Clinging to mercy, we fully embrace Your righteousness.

Captivated by Your love, we come as living sacrifices.
Your will, not ours; we surrender to Your purposes.
In love and zeal, we dedicate our hearts and minds.
Knowing You fill all and all, we bow in submission.
Immersed in unfailing love, we go forth in Your Love.

Captivated by Your love, we leave all traces of worldliness.
No longer friends with the world, consecrated, we pursue.
Your kingdom reigning, thoughts emerge, transforming.
The smell of darkness removed; new fragrances emerge.
Spreading Your fragrance, new life emerges everywhere.

Captivated by Your Love; destiny and purpose emerge.
In knowledge of Your will, enlightened, we press hard.
The past losing all significance, we press forward.
Conformed to Your death, in resurrection power, we tread.
Embracing Your cross heartily, we reach for what's ahead.

Captivated by Your Love, in holiness, we gain to attain.
Your fullness, yet to be revealed; we wait in anticipation.
The prize before us, Your love beckons to pursue eagerly.
Knowing we will be known as You are, we purify ourselves.
Longing for Your fullness revealed, we rejoice vehemently.

~

But you, O Lord, are a God of compassion and mercy, slow to get angry and filled with unfailing love and faithfulness.
Psalms 86:15 NLT

Treasures from the Heart's Portals

Looking to the heavens above, we reach for wisdom.
Hearing the voice of wisdom, we bow in humility.
Knowing Your word is truth, wisdom is given freely.
From heaven above, You speak softly to the heart.
With words of wisdom, treasures burst forth in part.

Hearing from above, we incline ears to wisdom.
Entering the heart's portals, wisdom bursts forth.
Faith stirring the heart, awakening infuses warmth.
Enlightenment igniting the mind, we await in stillness.
From heart portals opened, we run with goodness.

Expanding the heart, treasures pour forth in abundance.
Pumping treasures to the heart, faith rises with affluence.
The prize before us, Your love beckons to pursue eagerly.
His Word absorbed; affluence springs forth in all matters.
Faith coming by hearing; we expectantly listen intently.

Treasuring all given, strength and fortitude gain.
Endurance replenished, faith matures, embracing all pain.
Twists and turns spotted; we give way to invisible returns.
Unexpected treasures gracing, faith embraces all concerns.
All pertaining to life given, we rejoice in all returns.

∼

*Now to Him who can do exceedingly abundantly above all that we
ask or think, according to the power that works in us,
to Him be glory in the Church by Christ Jesus to all
generations, forever and ever. Amen.*
Ephesians 3:20

Bloom Where You're Planted

The breath of God touching, new life springs forth.
Intimately made in secret, our days He fashions.
Called according to His purposes, He steadily forms.
Knowing our beginning and ending, He plants.
Planted in His vineyard, He causes to flourish.

Submitting to His plans and purposes, we discern.
Looking up, His field of harvest, we recognize.
Embracing gifts and talents, we discern our places.
Whatever our hands find to do, we do mightily.
Knowing He sets us accordingly, we labor.

Testimonies intact, we sow faithfully in our fields.
While others standby, we give wholeheartedly.
In faith, love and purity, we seek not to offend.
Planted in His field, we flourish in all touched.
Harvests ripe, we labor and flourish in His courts.

In valleys of decision, multitudes wait to be chosen.
Harvests ripe, we direct laborers to plant and send.
Filling, overall, His glory settles on those who flourish.
Glory reconciling, multitudes convert and spring forth.
Breath of God touching; we stand together in unity.

∼

Do you not say, "There are still four months, and then comes the harvest? Behold, I say to you, lift up your eyes and look at the fields, for they are already white for harvest! The harvest truly is plentiful, but the laborers are few. Therefore, pray the Lord of the harvest to send out laborers into His harvest."
John 4:35 & Matthew 9:37-38

Innumerable Treasures of God

Flowing from His throne, we partake of His treasures.
Innumerable they are, we gaze as eternal possessors.
A foretaste of His treasures to come, we savor.
Bursting with revelation and insight, we favor.

Setting our hearts on that which is above, we gaze.
Peeking into His treasures innumerable, we hunger.
Through hardships, trials, and struggles, we endure.
Catching glimpses of eternal weights, we allure.

Hidden treasures revealed, we stand in assurance.
The promise to know eternal mysteries, we seek.
Wisdom and knowledge brimming, we encourage.
Partaking of innumerable mysteries, we engage.

Treasures Innumerable, claimed, He enriches freely.
The mind of Christ instructing, we do not lose hope.
Running the race, we focus on the joy set before us.
Embracing eternal weights, His treasures supply.

Called to seize, innumerable treasures inspire to action.
More than conquerors, we rise to conquer inaction.
Eternity in mind, nothing holding back, we dominate.
Treasures Innumerable, permeating the soul, we gain all.

~

The mystery which has been hidden from ages and from generations, but now has been revealed to His saints.
Colossians 1:26

From Despondency to Hope

Trusting in our own ways, we plan and scheme.
Filled with self-gloating and rejoicing, we daydream.
Given to self-centered, appealing choices, we squander.
Wallowing in regret and remorse, choices we ponder.

Reaping a life governed by self, we stand demoralized.
Caught in self-loathing, repercussions come our way.
Disenchanted, the soul weighed down in regret, we fret.
In depression, anxiety, and suicidal thoughts, we dismay.

Caught in webs of despondency, we look for rays of light.
In the distance, a light beckons for further exploration.
Light penetrating the soul, despair begins to dissolve.
Lifted from despair, heartened by the light, hope resolves.

Heartened and hopeful, we immerse ourselves in the light.
Light penetrating the heart, a gentle voice beckons.
Becoming clearer, He beckons to the invisible glimpsed.
Excitement taking over, weights lift in new perceptions.

Discovering an invisible kingdom, we give ourselves freely.
The voice revealed as the kingdom's King, we follow readily.
Filled with new purposes, new strategies, we envision.
Hearts fully engaged, we commit to His ways and decisions.

Choices, governed by kingdom perspectives, we thrive.
Enhanced by revelation, taken into deeper realms, we dive.
Given our mission and purpose, we delight in all gained.
Hope filling, we no longer wander, disenchanted with life.

∼

Peace, I leave with you, My peace I give to you; not as the world gives do I give to you. Let not your heart be troubled.
John 14:27

Love Comes to All

As the Father's only begotten, He comes to shower.
Though showering love on all, many don't respond.
Those receiving, He showers in love, now and forever.
While bound in sin, in love, He provides freedom.

Not willing any perish, He stands ready in love for all.
Embracing His cross, love flows through those believing.
Giving of ourselves heartedly, His love flows freely.
From one to another, love comes to all embracing.

Esteeming others more important; love flows freely.
In humility, one to another, treasures flow endlessly.
Laying down lives for others, healing comes to all.
Treasuring fruit over selfish gain, love comes to all.

Treasures flowing freely to all, He blesses abundantly.
Daily loaded with benefits, His love reigns triumphantly.
No longer trapped in self-serving, His Spirit Leads.
No longer steeped in sin and shame, blessings flow freely.

~

For God so loved the world that He gave His only begotten
Son that whoever believes in Him should not perish
but have everlasting life.
John 3:16

Fruit of the Spirit Treasured

Tasting precious fruit from God's presence, we ponder
Looking to others with expectation, we look with want.
Love, joy, peace, kindness, or gentleness, what's preferred?
With every kind of fruit tasted, He satisfied hungry hearts.

Whether self-control, or faithfulness, He satisfies.
Fully submitted to the Father's authority, He produces.
Looking to the Father above, He reveals His character.
Touched by His presence, fruit emanating, we treasure.

Giving birth to those believing, His seed matures.
Called to His likeness, His fruit, we treasure.
Looking to Him above, we fill with divine nature.
Submitting to Him above, His fruit, we treasure.

Whoever coming our way, the right fruit is available.
Treasuring spiritual fruit; He continually produces.
Produces for those in need, we discipline ourselves.
In self-control, and faithfulness, we seek to bless.

~

But the fruit of the Spirit is love, joy, peace, longsuffering, kindness, goodness, faithfulness, gentleness, self-control. Against such, there is no law.
Galatians 5:22-23

The Unfailing Love of the Father

Hurt, wounded, offended, we cry out in agony.
Lost in a maze of confusion, we stop and consider.
Gone too far to turn back, we bow in surrender.
Not bowing to bitterness that defiles, we yield.
Nowhere to go but forward, we pick up our shield.

Weakened by doubt and unbelief, we don't give in.
Knowing He never forsakes, we find comfort in Him.
Strengthening ourselves, we make straight paths.
Knowing too much to turn back, we step carefully.
Trusting the Father's unfailing love, we take courage.

Pursuing peace with all, we let go of all that offends.
Knowing He alone has the words of life, we take heart.
Looking back to past victories, seeds of faith sprout.
Reminded of the Father's unfailing love, we take heart.
As seeds of faith sprout, hope inspires fresh starts.

Looking for security, we trust in Him to restore.
Newness coming upon us, He renews to soar.
Surprised by His unfailing love, we treasure.
Sympathizing with our weakness, we boldly cling.
Not surprised by our weaknesses, confidence brims.

Received in full acceptance and forgiveness, faith arises.
Doubt and uncertainty diminished; freedom sets free.
No longer lost in confusion, we press forward mightily.
Gifts and calling restored, destiny releases purpose.
Restored, the past let go; we reach for what's ahead.

~

Your unfailing love, O Lord, is as vast as the heavens;
Your faithfulness reaches beyond the clouds.
Psalm 36:5 NLT

Treasures of Love and Mercy

In Your presence, we delight ourselves in You.
You alone are the One pouring Love and Mercy.
In Your love, You gave us a faithful High Priest.
You gave the One who delights in Love and Mercy.
Sympathizing with our weaknesses, You forgive all.

Who are we that You gave the One who gave all?
Embracing the cross, led to the slaughter, Your Son died.
Humiliated, scorned, beaten, and crucified, He gave all.
For our sins, He became sin so we could be righteous.
As a merciful, faithful High Priest, He embraced our sin.

As You have given Love and Mercy, we now offer.
Filling our hearts with treasures, we give ourselves.
In truth and righteousness, we pour into others.
So, others may know of Your great love, we embrace.
Embracing the cross, denying ourselves, we give.

His name lifted for all to see; He draws unto You.
Others coming to Him who gave all, we rejoice.
Knowing You will mold them as well, we give praise.
Love and mercy filling all bowing, we rejoice.
Filled with Your treasures, we give thanks.

~

But God who is rich in mercy, because of His great love with which He loved us, made us alive together with Christ (by grace you have been saved), and raised us up together, and made us sit together in the heavenly places in Christ Jesus, that in the ages to come He might show the exceeding riches of His grace in His kindness toward us in Christ Jesus.
Ephesians 2:4-7

The Holy Spirit, Our Helper

Trapped in ideological swirling thoughts we inquire.
Looking for answers, in our ways, we grow weary.
Lost in confusion, we seek wisdom and advice.
Calling on our Helper above, He comes readily,
Never leaving nor forsaking, we embrace heartily.

Ready and willing, He comes in wisdom and truthfulness.
Taking our hand, He reveals the path to fruitfulness.
Acknowledging Him in all our ways, He teaches to trust.
Filled with assurance, we press forward in illuminance.
Relinquishing authority to Him, we go forth in compliance.

Intimately acquainted with us, He guides unswervingly.
Given to reliance on Him daily, He speaks decisively.
Aware He never leaves nor forsakes; we boldly embrace.
No longer lost in confusion, we trust Him as counselor.
Confidence restored; we acknowledge Him as Helper.

When circumstances pull down, He's there to be found.
With just a touch, He plants our feet on solid ground.
From His place, treasures pour forth with affluence.
Seated with Christ, eternal treasures reveal in abundance.
From this perspective, He lifts above all that stumbles.

Hearts set on things above, He relieves the weight.
Eternal weights of glory glimpsed; we don't lose heart.
Thoughts and actions in sync, He strengthens daily.
Knowing we have such a Helper; we do all efficiently.
Advantages given we're more than conquerors in Christ.

~

Nevertheless, I tell you the truth. It is to your advantage that I go away; for if I do not go away, the Helper will not come to you; but if I depart, I will send Him to you.
John 14:7

Strength and Courage in Him

Drowning in fear, coming up for air, we veer.
Weakened by circumstances beyond control, we fear.
Afraid to step into the unknown, we stand paralyzed.
To be rid of fear that disables, we turn to Him above.
With words of encouragement, He stands by in love.

No longer willing to tolerate indifference, we pray.
Bound in worry and doubt, we seek release to slay.
Loss of ambition and initiative, for His help, we cry.
Captivated by fear that strangles, we seek liberty.
Forsaking unbelief, we seek freedom from captivity.

No longer willing to be self-absorbed, we embrace.
In Him who gives hope to all, we commit heartedly.
Instilling words of encouragement, we stand ready.
Believing He delivers from all, we embrace mightily.
Breathing deeply, we allow His words to transform.

Transforming our thoughts, His ways, we embrace.
Transformation taking hold, courage nourishes.
Filled with the Spirit, we press on in faith to serve.
Bold as a lion, fear left behind, we break the chains.
In His sufficiency, we press courageously to gain.

~

When I am afraid, I will trust in You. In God (I will praise His Word), In God I have put my trust; I will not fear. What can flesh do to me? For God has not given us a spirit of fear, but of power and of love and of a sound mind.
Psalm 56:3-4 & 2 Timothy 1:7

Treasured Stones Found

As treasured stones, we seek to be found.
From the heavens above, He looks down.
Those with understanding, He finds.
Grace filling, we present ourselves.
Giving sacrificially, we offer to Him above.

Built together as treasured stones, we co-labor.
Aligned with His blueprint, His measure produces.
Though secure, we prepare for what's ahead.
Stormy weather on the horizon, we build accordingly.
Sacrificing for one another, we press joyfully.

As treasured stones, an anointing is sought to discover.
Perilous times coming, greater measures given to fulfill.
Knitted together in His love, His measure increases in all.
His measure increasing in all the world, many are drawn.
Built together, His fullness rests upon treasured stones.

As faithful treasured stones, we glorify Him who chooses.
With hearts of gratitude, we give praise to Him who rescues.
Glory settling, we continually seek Him above to proclaim.
Knowing His coming is imminent, we run with hearts aflame.
Looking for the great day, we give of ourselves to reclaim.

Coming to Him as to a living stone, rejected indeed by men,
but chosen by God and precious, you also as living stones,
are being built up a spiritual house, a holy priesthood,
to offer up spiritual sacrifices acceptable to God
through Jesus Christ.
1 Peter 2:4-5

Delighting in the Lord's Presence

Strolling through the pathways of life, we partake.
All that's seen and heard, we look to Him above.
Discovering His presence in what's seen, we delight.
Hearing heightened, senses exploding, He reveals.
Knowing He views us with great delight, we enjoy.

Treasuring His thoughts, we give ourselves to Him.
Giving ourselves to Him heartedly, we sing praises.
Praise touching the heart, delighting in Him grows.
His thoughts filling mind and heart, joy explodes.
The joy of the Lord turning to strength, all is enjoyed.

His path filled with pleasures forever; we delight.
Amid trials, we delight, embracing His faithfulness.
From strength to strength, faith in Him pours forth.
From Faith to Faith, treasures revealed, joy increases.
Great delight in all discovered, we press forward.

Empowered by His presence shown in all, we bow.
In humility, we bow to Him, who abundantly satisfies.
Grace and mercy given in affluence; we give Him glory.
Thankful for strength and courage given, we press on.
Looking to eternal treasures to come, nothing prevents.

~

*Delight yourself also in the Lord, and He shall
give you the desires of your heart.*
Psalm 37:4

From Heaven Above

From heaven above, looking down, He sees all.
Aware He sees all, we sing joyfully in His presence.
With praise on our lips, we lift our hearts to Him.
Praise filling our hearts, we know He delights in us.
Looking upon us with great affection, He replenishes.

From heaven above, His Word in our hearts, He spies.
Knowing His Word is true, we allow it to transform.
His Word transforming, He fills us with understanding.
Discerning His filling, we fully embrace love in return.
Given freely to His Word and Spirit, we delight in Him.

His treasures hidden in our hearts; He watches with joy.
Watching all we do; He encourages when we stumble.
Unfailing love securing, we get up without condemnation.
Joyfully embracing His arms, He affirms and sympathizes.
From His throne of grace, He pours from His mercy.

From His dwelling, looking down, He sees all humanity.
Paying attention to all we do; He blesses with reassurance.
Eyes on all who fear Him, He fills with hope and assurance.
Unfailing love, delivering from oppression, He stirs trust.
Acting as a shield from all that's against us, we rejoice.

The Lord looks down from heaven upon the children of men
to see if there are any who understand who seek God.
Psalm 14:2

Waiting on the Lord

Waiting on the Lord, we keep lamps fully lit.
With strength and vitality, we press to outwit.
Mounting on the wings of an eagle, we don't faint.
Spirit led; we soar free without constraint.

With hearts of expectation, we embrace all decreed.
The Father's heart searched, He reveals what's needed.
Waiting on the Lord, He lavishly pours into our hearts.
Divine nature revealing, greatness is known in all parts.

Belief and confession rising, faith meets in expectance.
Acknowledging God in all ways, He call to repentance.
Trusting in Him, He brings to pass our hidden desires.
Submitted, we make straight paths for what He requires.

Presenting prayers and petitions, He heartily hears.
Praying without ceasing, our minds stay on Him.
With a still, small voice, we give ear to His mysteries.
Obediently responding in faith, He leads to victories.

Waiting patiently, gifts arrive for serving and ministry.
Attentive to the needs of others, we wait in symmetry.
In serving and waiting, grace flows in new dimensions.
Soaring to new heights, in His wind, He strengthens.

~

But those who wait on the LORD shall renew their strength; they shall mount up with wings like eagles; they shall run and not be weary; they shall walk and not faint.
Isaiah 40:31

Hearts Aflame

From the Holy Spirit, we seek to discover.
To achieve, we ask and knock to uncover.
Destined to be flames of fire, we breathe.
Blowing on the embers, our sparks ignite.
As the heart inflames, in Him, we delight.

Given to His will, we move in His sufficiency.
In His proficiency, faith explodes into flames.
Faith activated; ministry opportunities appear.
Enriched in flames, we turn to God for more.
Delighted in His manifested presence, we hear.

Filled with ignited passion, sparks inflame many.
Caught in the moment, others are reaped in plenty.
No longer feeding on useless things, we partake.
Fervency driven; His Spirit pours in abundance.
Given to the wind, gifts flow with His presence.

Fully developed, flames of fire, we will be.
Harvest fields, we go, igniting fires everywhere.
Gifts released; hearts everywhere catch fire.
Harvest fields white for harvest, laborers multiply.
Giving God glory for gifts given, we stand humbled.

~

"Do you not say, 'There are still four months and then comes the harvest'? Behold, I say to you, lift up your eyes and look at the fields, for they are already white for harvest! And he who reaps receives wages, and gathers fruit for eternal life, that both he who sows and he who reaps may rejoice together."
John 4:35-36 & John 4:35-36

Intimately Acquainted with God

Intimately acquainted with HIs ways, He's forevermore.
Knowing thoughts, dreams, fears, sins, He restores.
Wherever we go, nothing hidden, yet His love remains.
Towards us, His thoughts are more than can be numbered.
Brought into captivity, our thoughts, unencumbered.

May we know God as He's known us, even in our sins.
With His greatness beyond discovery, we seek to begin.
In His Word and creation, hidden keys reveal His majesty.
Hidden treasures discovered, we search with persistence.
Intimacy revealed, we seek Him without resistance.

In seeking and discovery, misconceptions disappear.
Teaching us, the Holy Spirit reveals His nature, so near.
Pondering beauty and majesty, He reveals ascriptions.
In His Word, we search out His divine distinctions.
By His Spirit, we press to uncover His depictions.

In wonder of His creation, His handiwork is discovered.
In beauty and magnificence, His creative zeal is uncovered.
In discovery, He's seen and known in all He's created.
Myriads of stars, streams, mountains, and waterfalls reveal.
In beauty and majesty, He's detected by all who kneel.

In omniscience, He knows the future and paths we take.
Going before as a guiding light, He knows what's at stake.
Trusting in Him, we navigate through dangers and setbacks.
With thoughts of peace, He fills us with faith and hope.
With more discovered, He reveals excellence for His sake.

Incomprehensible, He's inexhaustible in power succeeding.
In omnipotence, nothing is too difficult in power exceeding.
Performing and doing the hard things, our part is attainable.
Not minimizing His power, all things are obtainable.
In knowing, we discover we're linked to His divine ability.

In all that's created, in His eternal Godhead, He portrays.
Without excuse, we stand as sun, moon, and stars display.
Living and moving in Him, we experience greater intimacy.
As the sun, moon, and stars portray, we reflect His grandeur.
Knowing He's everywhere, we discover His splendor.

~

Oh LORD, You have searched me and known me, You know my sitting down and my rising up; You understand my thought afar off. You comprehend my path and my lying down and are acquainted with all my ways.
Psalm 139:1-3

Pressing Forward in Faith

With contrite hearts, we stand with ears to hear.
In promises given, we stand ready to possess.
Faith coming by hearing, our hearts draw near.
Breaking up the fallow ground, the seed, He imparts.
With the seed planted, roots go deep into our hearts.

Unbelief departing, in His power, we believe.
Word of faith imbedded; we stand in agreement.
Faith possessing, we subdue, pressing forward.
Choosing to believe in the Scripture, we receive.
With all things about life promised, we conceive.

God overseeing all, we respond accordingly.
Never leaving or forsaking, we press continually.
From faith to faith, obedience carries forward.
Giving according to needs, benefits flow freely.
Surprising us at how well He cares, we're blessed.

Blessed beyond measure, we enjoy all springing forth.
Pressed and shaken together, running over, He blesses.
Faith imparting, He continually reveals His treasures.
Constantly aware of our needs, He rewards faithfulness.
Living by faith, we enjoy His righteousness in all things.

∼

Brethren, I do not count myself to have apprehended; but one thing I do, forgetting those things which are behind and reaching forward to those things which are ahead, I press toward the goal for the prize of the upward call of God in Christ Jesus.
Philippians 3:13-14

Multiplying What's Sown

Laying treasures at His feet, hearts inflame.
Multiplying what's sown, we bless in His name.
From heaven's abundance, freely, we bestow.
From His gifts, our offerings freely flow.

Freely given, blessings in abundance flourish.
Revelation lifting, illumination nourishes.
Transformed, we clear our self-centered ways.
New ways obeyed; He brighten all our days.

Unburdened, we give generously, with cheer.
From hearts sowing deep, our joy is sincere.
Liberality enriching, we generously share.
Sowing and reaping in joy, His glory appears.

With sufficiency in all, we minister,
Abounding, we hear constant whispers.
From faith to faith, Your righteousness lights.
In kingdom purposes, He gives insight.

Treasures merging in Him, we reap,
His divine nature within, we go deep.
Into the fields of harvest, joyfully we stride,
From His resources, planting grows wide.

We stay joyful in all, whether low or high.
Grace abundantly supplied, steadily we ply.
Fruits of righteousness increasing, we sing.
A harvest rich with joy, thanksgiving rings.

With seeds multiplying, we give with glee,
Hearts crowned in joy, His love we see.

~

*But this I say: He who sows sparingly will also reap sparingly,
and he who sows bountifully will also reap bountifully.*
2 Corinthians 9:6

Shifting Paradigms

Glory to glory, in new paradigms, the Lord assimilates.
New patterns placed, captivity to His Word liberates.
Old patterns destroyed; liberty emerges in the Spirit.
Guidance given, what's next is embraced without limit.

New habits established; fruit abundantly appears.
Paradigms shifting, false premises disappear.
Spirit strong, strongholds disintegrate without agitation.
Righteous strongholds gracing, foundations strengthen.

Paradigms shifting, fresh vision catapults to destiny.
God's glory gifting, talents come freely with clarity.
Gifts differing in proportion to faith, vision releases.
Ministering in God's ability, His presence increases.

New paradigms taking hold, the puzzle comes together.
Distinctive pieces revealed, the picture becomes clearer.
Recognizing value in others, each piece finds its place.
His body emerging, value releasing, His Spirit gives grace

Ministering in Spirit more glorious, righteousness exceeds.
Seeing ourselves transformed into His image, He leads.
Esteeming others in Christ, His presence is more evident.
Transformation evidenced; His body becomes excellent.

~

Now, the LORD is the Spirit, and where the Spirit of the LORD is, there is liberty. But we all, with unveiled face, beholding as in a mirror the glory of the LORD, are being transformed into the same image from glory to glory, just as by the Spirit of the LORD.
2 Corinthians 3:17-18

The Voice of the Sentry

Birthed into this world as babes, we enter with innocence.
Seeing and perceiving, we look in wonder with dissonance.
Perceptions formed, we fill with assumptions and confusion.
Caught in meaningless existence, we cry out in desperation.
Lost in confusion and anxiety, we grope for a ray of light.

Blindness gripping, we hope in the dark of the night.
Clutter stiflingly, a still, small voice speaks with difference.
Questioning, we investigate its origin and significance.
Speaking with warmth amid turmoil and unease, we question.
Given to expectation, we wait in anticipation with discretion.

In moments of stillness, we stand with hearing ears.
In anticipation, we wait to capture that moment of peace.
Hearing again, the voice penetrates, pointing to a path.
With hearing ears, the voice beckons to the path ahead.
Eyes riveted, light rests on something blocking the path.

Eyes and ears riveted; a cross blocks the path's entry.
Speaking with clarity its purpose, the sentry explains.
With understanding opened, we embrace it unstained.
Sweetness emanating from His voice, entrance is gained.
Peaceful obedience flooding, other voices are silenced.

Embracing the cross in humility, our thoughts adjust.
Carrying it everywhere, the sentry's voice, we trust.
Oh, the thrill of adventure as He leads, filled with joy.
Confident, unafraid of what's ahead, we reach to attain.
Burdens and the cares relieved, in peace, we now reign.

No longer a sentry but a friend, He walks alongside, guiding.
Now assisting, He fills our hearts with peace and assurance.
Whispering, He says, "Let us walk together as co-laborers."
No longer in confusion, we embrace the cross shown, daily.
Knowing He leads to adventures; we walk together joyfully.

Committing to Him daily, He leads to purposes now shown.
Filled with love, joy, and peace, He daily loads with benefits.
Meaningless existence obliterated; there's no need to pretend.
No longer groping in the dark, the path grows lighter and brighter.
Giving thanksgiving, His sweet presence lingers, walking together.

However, when He, the Spirit of truth, has come, He will guide you into all truth; for He will not speak on His own authority, but whatever he hears, He will speak; and He will tell you things to come. He will glorify Me, for He will take of what is Mine and declare it to you.
John 16:13-14

Peace Amid Turbulence

Frustrated, lost in uncertainty, desperation stirs.
Hopeless, sinking fast; atmospheric assaulting explodes.
All seen and heard, brain fog reigns uncontrolled.
Gasping for air, sights set on cruciality, we ponder.

How senseless, berating those differing.
Lost in bickering, skirmishes linger in haze.
Peaceable among all, caustic air dissipates.
Discovering lost times, we awaken to stability.

Peace rescuing, turbulence gives way to strength.
Focusing on atmospheric goodness, darkness unravels.
Embracing newness, uncertainty dead, we unshackle.
Mobility restored; life's purpose enlightens.

Free to soar, limitless, we tread in life's adventures.
Hope restored, enjoyment accompanying, we live freely.
No longer alarmed, thoughts give space to others.
Respecting one another, regardless, we live peaceably.

~

*But know this, that in the last days perilous times will come:
For men will be lovers of themselves, lovers of money, boasters,
proud, blasphemers, disobedient to parents, unthankful, unholy,
unloving, unforgiving, slanderers, without self-control, brutal,
despisers of good, traitors, headstrong, haughty, lovers of
pleasure rather than lovers of God.*
2 Timothy 3:1-4

Avoiding Foolish Chatter

Imaginations given over to false perceptions, many conspire.
Armed and dangerous, they drag others into foolish chatter.
Wrapped in false illusions, they trip and stumble through life.
Trapped by deceit, giving voice to foolish thoughts, they weigh.
Spinning in whirlwinds of unrighteous activity, they fall prey.

For the love of foolish chatter, they fool the gullible.
Many desiring to have ears tickled, become destructible.
Filled with lies and half-truths, they're bound with contempt.
Fear as a weapon, they come, lies leading to bondage.
Without discernment, they become lost in illusions.

Shattered, broken vessels; foolish chatter disintegrates.
The arrival of the holy ones, they question foolishness.
Ears opened, spirits quieted, they question delusiveness.
Eyes opened; heavenly reality reveals the heart's treasures.
Exposed to light, filled with wonder, peace transposes.

Foolish chatter controlled; they cease to beguile.
The Spirit of truth given, they no longer trip and stumble.
Deceit unbound; they give voice to those entangled.
Rescuing those fallen prey, they speak words of comfort.
Whirlwinds of malice destroyed; they stand triumphant.

~

But avoid foolish and ignorant disputes, knowing that they generate strife. [24] *And a servant of the Lord must not quarrel but be gentle to all, able to teach, patient,* [25] *in humility correcting those who are in opposition, if God perhaps will grant them repentance, so that they may know the truth.*
2 Timothy 2:23-25

In You Alone

Trusting You alone, we lean upon Your Word and Spirit.
Your Word a lamp unto the path; we look to You alone.
You alone are the One giving direction to the weary.
Waiting on You alone, we drink daily from Your Spirit.
With Your word washing over, the mind renews daily.

In You alone, we rely upon, giving breath to revive.
Upon You, all burdens and cares cast, You relieve.
Waiting on You, divine ability flows as we believe.
In You alone, the weary mount on the wings of an eagle.
Seated in heavenly places, we soar to new heights.

Your Word filling, we fill with thoughts so fine.
The mind of Christ given; You immerse into all divine.
All things given concerning life and godliness, we dine.
Taking possession of Your divine nature, we press.
In You alone, we press to the upward call and prize.

Your precious promises filling, we escape to You alone.
The world's corruption no longer holding back, we soar.
In you, we adore forever walking together in Your love.
Now made complete and whole, Your love washes over.
Forever grateful, in Your presence, righteous we are.

~

Trust in the Lord with all your heart and lean not on your own
understanding; in all your ways acknowledge Him,
and He shall direct your paths.
Proverbs 3:5-6

Perfected in Righteousness

A lamb without blemish, He came for those defeated.
Perfect in all His ways, His righteousness exceeded.
Without sin, His Father's will, He pursued to free all.
Clothed in the righteousness of His Father, He bled.
Giving His life in all things, those defeated believed.

Embracing His cross wholeheartedly, He bled to save.
Becoming sin, He erased the sins of those who believe.
Crying out in agony, betrayed, and forsaken, He bled.
A lamb led to slaughter; He became our righteousness.
Giving up the ghost, He died a sinner's death for all.

Prevailing over death, rising from the dead, He overcame.
His righteousness now ours, we stand in His perfection.
Satan defeated; He gained the victory for all believing.
Believing in the power of His resurrection, we partake.
Because He was forsaken, we stand nurtured in hope.

Clothed in His righteousness, we embrace His cross.
Embracing His cross, we turn our hearts in repentance.
In the power of His resurrection, we leave sin behind.
Without sin and shame holding back, we pursue holiness.
Locked into His righteousness, we press to glorify.

Though perfected in righteousness, we trip and stumble.
Asking forgiveness, we receive Him as our substitute.
As a merciful High Priest, we run boldly into His arms.
Forgiving, He clothes in righteousness to fulfill His will.
Perfected forever, in righteousness, we overcome in all.

*For by one offering, He has perfected forever
those who are being sanctified.*
Hebrews 10:14

Embracing the Peace of God

From wayward ways, lost within, we moan.
From heaviness overwhelming, we stand alone.
Guilt and condemnation engulfing, we agonize.
From torment within, we pray for release.

Coming to take sin and shame, the Lamb comes.
In cleansing blood, we no longer suffer shame.
Peace flowing like a river, torment washes away.
Breathing new life, atonement extends to whomever.

Troublesome Problems, like a mighty tide, pull under.
Extending His hand, He delivers from crying blunder.
With just a touch, He relieves, securing in mercy.
Flooding our souls with peace, He rescues in wonder.

Flooded with uncertainty, anxiety rises to destroy.
Given to doubt, temptation gives way to compromises.
Embracing Him, trust celebrates Kingdom surprises.
Pursuing Him, peace comes surpassing understanding.

Giving praise, we thank Him for His perfect sacrifice.
Sympathizing with us, we come boldly into His presence.
We give praise to Him, who continually looks after us.
In unbelief, He readily forgives, putting us at ease.

~

*And the peace that surpasses all understanding will
guard your hearts and minds through Christ Jesus.*
Philippians 4:7

Quickened by His Word

Quickened by His Word, we exalt Him.
His word a lamp unto our feet, we run.
His commands, the apple of our eyes, we exalt.
Treasures quickened to our hearts, we enjoy.

Given to truth, we no longer go astray.
Obedient in all, He blesses beyond belief.
Granted the heart's treasures, we rejoice.
Quickened by His love, we press in admiration.

Quickened by His Word, we give testimony.
No longer bound by the past, we believe.
Embracing His word as truth, we delight.
His word cleansing our souls, we give thanks.

Meditating on His word and ways, we give praise.
Inspiration given; we delight in His Spirit.
Wholeheartedly following, we delight in all given.
Ordering our steps, He leads with precision.

Quickened by His Word, we seek His treasures.
Taking heed to His word, we no longer wander.
Confessing all given, treasures pour in abundance.
Filled with praise and thanksgiving, we rejoice.

~

A new commandment I give you, that you love one another; as I have loved you, that you also love one another.
John 13:34

Breaking Free to Run Freely

Wounded, broken, gasping for air, we struggle to be free.
Filled with pain and anxiety, lost in confusion, we suffer.
Screaming in uncontrollable anger, rage releases to offend.
Mistreated, abused, ignored, stuck in denial, we carry on.
Drowning in self-destruction, we languish without hope.

In despair, blinded by deception and injustice, we struggle.
Knowing no other way to move forward, we give into apathy.
Disillusioned, groping in blindness, we struggle to be free.
Not knowing what to do, we look for rays of hope.
In the distance beyond hearing, a voice is heard in the wind.

Reminded of similar voices from the past, we strain to hear.
With a glimmer of hope, faith as a mustard seed gives birth.
The voice becoming more robust, we press to hear more.
Drawing attention to the festering wound, the voice motions.
Knowing the horror of the wound, fear drowns the voice.

Not willing to let go, the voice draws closer in empathy.
Not willing to lose touch, we give ear in desperation.
Responding to empathy given, we dare to peel the scab.
With gentle encouragement, the voice soothing, we peel.
Overcoming a rush of fear, confidence surges with hope.

Empowered with new confidence, faith rises to break free.
Openly acknowledging the wound's ugliness, healing begins.
With a surge of faith, the voice enters, revealing Himself.
Known as the Holy Spirit, He comes showing the way.
Empowered to break free from all binding, we submit.

Embracing promises for healing and overcoming, we press.
Forgetting the past, clean slate given, we make straight paths.
With hands lifted, we look to Him above, who sets free.
Confidence and assurance brewing, healing takes hold.
Darkness dissipating, in new-found freedom, we rejoice.

Running with endurance, we fill with vision and purpose.
Vision filling, destiny opening, fill with peace and joy.
Strengthened in God by joy, past wounds fade in significance.
Thankful for the voice in the wind beckoning, we give praise.
The prize before us, we give ourselves to Him who beckons.

~

Do you not know that those who run in a race all run,
but one receives the prize? Run in such a way
that you may obtain it.
1 Corinthians 9:24

Hearts Freely Committed

Saved to God's purposes, we're drawn.
Hearts engaged, we come with expectations.
Tasting His goodness, we commit to Him.
Hearts filled with hunger, we ask for more.

What is it that's required, we ask?
Hearts freely and totally committed.
What does it entail and cost, we ask?
As living sacrifices, we count the cost.

From heaven, He observes those seeking.
Will we be those He finds, we wonder?
Ready to discover what's ahead, we engage.
With hearts set on His purposes, we rejoice.

Hearts fully engaged; we discover His gifts.
Behaving like Christians, we walk in obedience.
Being patient in tribulation, we count it all joy.
Sensitive to needs of others, we embrace freely.

No longer bound to sin, we flee from worldliness.
Decisions based on kingdom realities; we rejoice.
Walking circumspectly, we redeem time for Him.
Freely and totally committed, we relish His love.

~

*I beech you therefore, brethren, by the mercies of God,
that you present your bodies a living sacrifice, holy acceptable to
God, which is your reasonable service, and do not be conformed
to this world, but be transformed by the renewing of your mind,
that you may prove what is that good and
acceptable and perfect will of God.*
Romans 12:1-2

Awakened by the Sunrise

Rising from the East, the sun awakens our senses.
Clouds expressing glory reveal its magnificence.
As colors emanate beauty, our hearts refresh.
Reminded of God's love, our hearts rejoice.

Awakened to His magnificence, we rise.
Enlightened by His presence, we give praise.
Opening our hearts to Him, we prepare.
His Son shining brightly, we give praise.

Awakened by His beauty, we look to Him above.
Given to His magnificence, we revel in His love.
His Son rising in our hearts, we give praise.
His Spirit immersing, we rise in obedience.

Called to emanate His glory, we rise to behold.
His Son rising in our hearts, we sense His power.
Refreshed and renewed in His beauty, He empowers.
The Son emanating from within, His beauty spreads.

Awakened from slumber, we rise to proclaim.
His Son rising in our hearts, His power we reclaim.
Given freely to His Spirit, we rise as His flames.
As flames of fire, His anointing spreads His fame.

~

From the rising of the sun to its going down
The Lord's name is to be praised.
Psalm 113:3

Looking to God in all Things

Looking to God in all things, we wait expectantly for His promises.
Seeking diligently, we labor together for His treasures to abound.
Given wisdom from above, we yield to Him, who supplies our needs.
Looking to Him in His sufficiency, accordingly, we strive as He adds.
Adding to our faith, He fills our hearts with treasures from above.

Looking to God in all, we stretch forth in obedience for virtue.
Strengthened through stretching and straining, we rejoice in truth.
Pressing forward, we give ourselves to Him, who fills all in all.
As truth takes hold, freedom from what once bound releases.
With freedom from past bondages, we run freely and vigorously.

Looking to God for wisdom, His Spirit directs in all things.
With obedience to His Word, understanding enlightens.
With the knowledge of His will, we're free to pursue destiny.
During difficulty, gaining knowledge, treasures pour forth.
As peace and surety take hold, hope in Him anchors our souls.

Looking to Him in self control, fleshly desires are in check.
Kept in check, we don't get bogged down in worthlessness.
Responding to His promptings, we flow freely in His purposes.
Filled with zeal towards His plans, we delight in His working.
Expressing His character in all, self-control leads victoriously.

Looking to God, adding perseverance to faith, we overcome.
Perseverance in place, difficulties, and opposition won't hinder.
Pressing forward in opposition, Satan in check, we obtain victory.
No longer bound by failure and insecurity, we press forward.
Persevering under pressure, His Spirit reigns liberally for gain.

Looking to Him alone in godliness, we rise above all that defames.
With pure devotion, He sees those given wholly to His purposes.
Hearts purely devoted; He embraces with His Sovereignty.
Given to His sovereign purposes, in pure devotion, we sing praises.
Fruitful in godliness, gifts spill forth abundantly for His purposes.

Looking to Him for brotherly kindness, treasures extend to all.
Compassionate and unselfish, brotherly kindness reigns abundantly.
Generous to all coming our way, we extend His blessings.
For those passing our way, friendliness leaves a kind fragrance.
Filled with warm-heartedness, brotherly kindness ignites others.

~

Therefore, brethren, be even more diligent to make your call and election sure, for if you do these things, you will never stumble; for so an entrance will be supplied to you abundantly into the everlasting kingdom of our Lord and Savior Jesus Christ.
1 Peter 1:10-11

Lights Amid the Darkness

Called from the world to be conquerors, we pray.
Given wisdom from above, we seek enlightenment.
In a world with hate, violence, and ignorance, we pray.
Glimpsing what our carnal eyes perceive, we dismay.
Setting our hearts on that which is above, Hope sways.

Darkness descending, perception fights to secure.
Security needed, thoughts turn upward to ensure.
Seeking to decipher the way, we acknowledge.
Acknowledging Him in our ways, we seek assurance.
Obedient to His ways, He directs with reassurance.

No longer wise in self, we gain new senses of visibility.
Spiritual eyes opened wide; peace brings feasibility.
New possibilities rising, faith meets new challenges.
Revelation replacing fear, we disregard all that terrifies.
No longer wallowing in paranoia, we rise to rectify.

Rising as conquerors in all, we give ourselves openly.
The harvest ripe, we labor setting free from darkness.
Empowered by His greatness, treasures release publicly.
Through darkness and deceit, we invade releasing light.
Shining lights amid the darkness, multitudes are gleaned.

~

Arise, shine; for our light has come! And the glory of the Lord is risen upon you. ² For behold, the darkness shall cover the earth, and deep darkness the people; but the Lord will arise over you, and His glory will be seen upon you.
Isaiah 60:1

Breakthrough to the Invisible Realm

With natural eyes, we stumble, into stagnation.
Discovered, a realm exists without observation.
Freed to the invisible realm, we flee for what's pure.
Escaping darkness, we flee, dwelling safe and secure.

Armor given, protective shields appear for security.
Trampling on evil's power, freedom exercises authority.
In His secret place, we cling to Most High in surety.
Armor protecting paths revealed, we discover ability.

Taking the Son's hand, He fills with confidence.
Perception unlocked; we walk in His providence.
Lighting our paths; His light inspires to proficiency.
Trusting, we no longer lean upon our sufficiency.

Faith in kingdom substance unseen, we reign.
In testing, we cling to His Word in obedience.
Treasuring His Word, we press in persistence.
Seemingly disappearing, we hold fast, pressing,

Mountains removed, nothing stopping, we press on.
Elation for what's ahead, we proceed in anticipation.
Faith tested, we know we will come forth as gold.
In the Father's love, He never forsakes in all told.

Reigning in the invisible, we're secure in God's love.
Plans and purposes birthed; realities come from above.
Looking for heaven's city, we discover the builder above.
Revelation given, it's more magnificent than imagined.

~

That the God of our Lord Jesus Christ, the Father of glory, may give to you the Spirit of wisdom and revelation in the knowledge of Him, the eyes of your understanding being enlightened;
Ephesians 1:15-16

The Kingdom Powered Life

Not of this world, leaning on Him, we live and reign.
Thoughts shaped by His Word; we press hard to gain.
Spiritually enriched, we seek Him and His Kingdom first.
With spiritual eyes fully opened, His treasures disperse.

Faith in Him, we feed on His goodness in abundance.
Committing to His ways, thoughts fill with substance.
Faith in His Word and promises, we lay hold to prove.
Listening to the heart, the mind directs our moves.

Called to His purposes, we walk with tenacity.
In sync in purpose, He fills with vision and destiny.
With desires realized, we serve enthusiastically.
In awe of His blessings, faith renews ecstatically.

Holding fast to Him, we treasure His Word in all told.
A deeper sense of His ways, we come forth as gold.
Rich in His grace, we cling to Him during testing in all.
In joy and resolve, we press forward to the upward call.

Governed by stewardship, we give to His causes faithfully.
When draws are needed, we willingly give cheerfully.
Casting bread upon the water, we reap as faith unfolds.
Loaded with benefits, His kingdom authority takes hold.

Abasing or abounding, we give thanks in all measures.
For peace that guards hearts and minds, we give thanks.
To Him who supplies, He makes rich by His treasures.
He who causes triumph, we give glory in all adventures.

~

Therefore, do not worry, saying, 'What shall we eat?' or 'What shall we wear?' For after all these things, the Gentiles seek. But seek first the kingdom of God and His righteousness, and all these things shall be added to you.
Matthew 6:31-33

Faith Erupts

Sometimes, coming to You, there's a fog of unbelief.
Without condemnation, You're always there giving relief.
Trusting in You, faith washes over our spirits, unstopped.
Reminded of Your greatness, thoughts stay focused.
Your love washing over our troubled souls, faith erupts.
Amid circumstances pulling down, unbelief corrupts.

Looking downward, we're blinded to what's promised.
Like distant mountains, Your promises stand true.
Eyes refocused, You free from the molehills of unbelief.
Lifting eyes to all You've promised, faith erupts.

Problems conflicting with Your Word, unbelief settles in.
In confusion and delusion, we fall prey to false perceptions.
In agreement with Your Word, peace overrides within.
Humbly admitting wrong perceptions, we trust Your Word.
Faith and trust in the Word's purity placed, faith erupts.

At times, turning, there's no sense of Your presence.
Unbelief tempting, darkness grips as visibility ceases.
Holding to Your steps, in faith we walk, laying hold.
With light shining ahead, we come forth as gold.
Treasuring Your word more than food, faith erupts.

Without vision, casting off restraint, unbelief corrupts.
With renewed vision and purpose, eyes open wide.
Engaging with Your Spirit, we walk side by side.
Given to strange conquests, we don't lose heart.
Communicating what's perceived, faith erupts.

~

For in it the righteousness of God is revealed from faith to faith;
as it is written, "The just shall live by faith.
Romans 1:17

As the Wheel Turns

As the wheel turns, the potter shapes for peculiarity.
With marred clay, He shapes with wisdom and clarity.
As clay in His hands, so are we as He takes pleasure.
Delighting at the wheel, He creates marvelously.
The wheel turning, He shapes each vessel uniquely.

As the wheel turns, He shapes to for vision and purpose.
Accordingly, the potter arranges His chosen vessels.
With precision, He shapes for their intended use.
Knowing their future, how each respond, He shapes.
The wheel turning, He fashions with eternal purposes.

As the wheel turns, in mercy, He allows for weaknesses.
Recognizing imperfections in all, He continues to shape.
With perfect views of their end, He shapes accordingly.
Knowing whether unto honor or not, He molds.
The wheel turning, there's sadness for those who resist.

As the wheel turns, not knowing as He knows, we ponder.
Catching glimpses of His hands at work, we become pliable.
Carefully watching His vessels in action, the potter smiles.
Setting up divine appointments, He chooses wisely for all.
The wheel turning, He shapes as tasks are completed.

As the wheel turns, the chosen fully embrace their potter,
Delighting in the potter's work, they energetically go forth.
With anticipation, pressing through obstacles, they trust.
Aware the potter is intimately acquainted, faith arises.
The wheel turning, growth and maturity are recognized by all.

O house of Israel, can I not do with you as this potter?"
says the Lord. "Look, as the clay is in the potter's hand,
so are you in My hand, O house of Israel!
Jeremiah 18:6

Homeward Bound

As pilgrims marching toward the eternal city, we look.
Believing in Christ, our names are written in His book.
Leaving temporary things behind, we press forward.
Looking for the city, whose maker is God, He rewards.
The Invisible Kingdom in partial view, He transports.

Sacrificial Lamb given; the way clears to His throne.
Discovering the way, He reveals our eternal home.
Giving ourselves to His sacrifice, the path we uncover.
Believing in His Son, Jesus, the gateway, we discover.
Giving thanks, our eternal home's beauty uncovers.

Clothed in majesty, He comes to set up His throne.
With promises fulfilled, He prepares a place to be shown.
With eyes and ears seeing and hearing, beauty awaits.
According to our desires, the Great Architect mandates.
Clothed with celestial bodies, we reign in the unknown.

The sting of death removed, we rejoice forevermore.
In healing waters, without pain or sorrow, we adore.
Bearing the image of the heavenly, He raises incorruptible.
In the twinkle of an eye, we're changed, indestructible.
In His presence, He gives joy with pleasures forevermore.

Reunited with those who went before, we bask and savor.
With hearts filled with wonder, we explore and discover.
In beauty prepared, discovery surpasses imagination.
On streets paved in pure gold, we revel in celebration.
In all revealed, we revel in our inheritance, fully discovered.

∼

Let not your heart be troubled; you believe in God, believe also in Me. In My Father's house are many mansions; if it were not so, I would have told you. I go to prepare a place for you.
John 14:1-2

Caught in Pursuit of a Lost Soul
Ken's Testimony

In panic, crying out in desperation, I desired to be free.
Discovered in captivation, my life flashed before me.
Like a fish with a hook in its mouth, I was caught.
Not ready to submit, I fought the hook, trying to spit it out.
Jerking the line periodically, I knew You were still there.

Why do I run, fighting Your hook, resisting being captured?
Freight train hopping from place to place, I often wondered.
With the hook set, reeling me in periodically, I resisted.
Letting go, again and again, I returned to sin and stubbornness.
How long will Your patience last, I wondered, in my distress.

Breaking me, Your patience exhausted me, little by little.
Raging on, the battle for my soul continued in non-committal.
What was resisted? Your unfailing love or fear of surrender?
Lost in a spiritual maze of philosophies, I stood in wonder.
What was discovered so long ago, drawing me so near?

Not giving in, stubbornly refusing, I stood in denial.
Lost in confusion, I desired but didn't quite know how.
Blindsided, caught in a hypnotic trance, I finally decided.
In a moment of intense struggle, worn out, I caved.
The battle over, You wrapped me in the arms of Your love.

Your patience taking opportunity, You waited to intercept.
Outwitting stubbornness and deception without force, You drew.
Leading to a moment of awe-inspiring revelation, my spirit leapt.
It was You I looked for all along. Why did I wait so distraught?
Forever grateful for Your pursuit of a lost soul, I was caught.

~

**Read Ken's complete testimony in his book,
"The Adventures of Space and Hobo."**

May God bless you Mightily by Becoming one of His lively Stones.

Knitted and framed together as lively stones, He builds.
As each stone discovers its gift, He places strategically.
Freely given to expression, we press on, building accordingly.
As each stone freely explores, His glory overshadows.
Bathed in glory, multitudes repent, changing dramatically.

*Coming to Him as to a living stone, rejected indeed by men,
but chosen by God and precious, you also as living stones,
are being built up a spiritual house, a holy priesthood, to
o offer up spiritual sacrifices acceptable to God
through Jesus Christ.*
1 Peter 2:4-5

About the Author

Ken Birks is an ordained Pastor/Teacher in the Body of Christ. He functions as an elder and is one of the teaching pastors at The Rock of Roseville in California. He is presently semi-retired with a writing ministry and serves as a wedding officiant in the Sacramento region. Before this, for twelve years, Ken was the Senior Pastor of Golden Valley Christian Center, a Spirit-filled, non-denominational church in Roseville.

Ken attended and graduated from the Charismatic Bible College of Anchorage. He came into a relationship with Apostle Dick Benjamin, then the Pastor of Abbott Loop Christian Center (ALCC) in Anchorage, Alaska.

Aside from The Lord Jesus Christ, the core of Ken's spiritual being and the person he's become is a direct result of the influence and teaching he received from Dick Benjamin for more than 25 years." Other influences have been Bob Mumford from Life Changers and, in the past 20+ years, Pastor Francis Anfuso of The Rock of Roseville.

Ken has been married to Lydia for 45 years plus. They have two adult children and consider them their highest calling, along with the many teens and children they have been foster or surrogate parents to over the past 30 plus years.

Learn more about Ken by checking out Ken's internet ministry, "Sowing Seeds of Faith," at kenbirks.com. Sowing Seeds of Faith reaches over 5500 unique visitors a month with free Bible studies, devotional poetry, sermon outlines, video messages, podcasts, and other Bible study materials to help equip saints for the work of the ministry.

Other Books by Ken Birks

Rise of the Anointed Ones

Ken Birks has written a masterpiece of superb continuity. Each devotional stands on its own, but together, they propel you into a rewarding journey of experiencing God's presence in tumultuous times. The majestic flow from theme to theme contains powerful prophetic revelation as God calls His end-time warriors to arise. The poems that follow each devotional are Davidic and musical. This book is like a voice in the wilderness calling God's beloved away from all that distracts Him who is jealous for His bride. – *Ed Becker and David Fredrickson*

Treasures From Above

These devotionals are designed to enhance your relationship with the Lord Jesus Christ in all aspects of your walk. The intent is to draw you into a deeper understanding of how the Holy Spirit and God's Word work together to conform you to the image of Christ. Each devotional should inspire you to be all you can be in Christ as you embrace the wonderful promises of God to help you receive all that pertains to the life God has given you. The aspect that separates this book from other devotionals is that each devotional ends with a biblically inspired poem that encapsulates the essence of the devotional.

Other Books by Ken Birks

Prophetic Purposes and the Zeal of the Lord

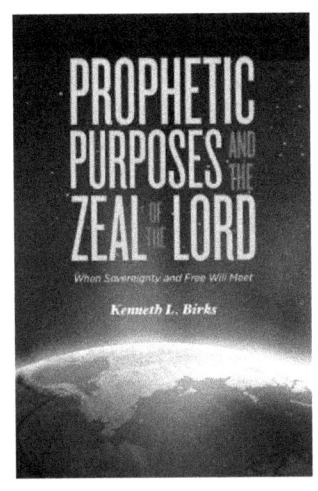

Do you believe worldwide revival is possible? Try to imagine what it will be like when the Church rises in the glory spoken of by the prophet, Isaih. Just as God, in His sovereignty, brought forth the Messiah according to Daniel's prophecy, He will bring forth the prophetic purpose of a worldwide revival according to His timing. God's people, whom He planted in every city, village, town, and countryside worldwide, will stand up as a vast army, just as Ezekiel prophesied. His prophetic purpose will be fulfilled. As God breathes on the dry bones prophesied by the prophet Ezekiel, His glory will fill all in all, just as Paul prophesied to the Ephesians. This book explores and instructs how to be ready for this prophecy and others that God will fulfill before the coming of Christ to set up His eternal kingdom on earth as it is in heaven.

The Adventures of Space and Hobo

The Adventures of Space and Hobo tells the story of Ken's nomadic life after Vietnam. The book explores the on-the-ground confusion and chaos of the Vietnam War and its effects on a generation and those who served. Named "Space" by a new friend, Hobo, Ken and his traveling companion hit the road to partake of all the possibilities of that generation in search of adventure and uncharted experiences. The story

Other Books by Ken Birks

takes us step by step along the path of awakening a lost soul on his way to understanding himself, his path, and the meaning of his life.

The Journey: Discovering the Invisible Path

The journey gives you a glimpse into God's path for your life. Whether you are starting your journey in the middle or have detoured and lost your way, this book will help you. This practical guidebook will illuminate the invisible path that leads to God's goodness and experiencing His kingdom within. It will lead you to discover the most incredible adventure of your life.

Quote from Pastor Francis Anfuso
Ken simplifies complex concepts and masterfully unpacks the Bible's greatest mysteries. He provides a sure foundation for a lifetime of insight.

Workbooks by Ken Birks

Biblical Perspectives Course

This course features lessons designed to give you a solid Biblical foundation in the elementary truths of God's Word. It has three things in mind: building doctrinal foundations, developing godly character, and helping you discover and find God's destiny and purpose for your life. Please see the following website for more information and Lesson Titles:

www.kenbirks.com/perspectives-both/

Workbooks by Ken Birks

More Biblical Perspectives Course

This course features lessons focused on three major areas of our Christian growth: doctrine, character, and destiny.

These lessons are designed to give you biblical perspectives that strengthen your Christian foundation and help you walk with God more deeply.

Please see the following website for more information and lesson titles: www.kenbirks.com/perspectives-both/

Small-Group Lesson Guides

This guide includes twenty-five lessons that are foundational for discovering the life of Jesus in small group Bible studies.

Please see the following website for complete information and titles:

www.kenbirks.com/discipleship/lesson-guides.htm

Reviews and References

Richard C. Benjamin, Apostle, Pastor, Deceased

I have known my friend, Ken Birks, for 38 years. He is a man of absolute integrity. He is a diligent student of the Bible. He is a Holy Spirit-filled teacher. His books contain many scriptures referred to and identified in the pages. In short, his books are based on the Bible. Ken is also an example of his writing in his books. I recommend his books to individuals, small group leaders, pastors, churches, Bible schools, and seminaries. His book, The Journey, will help make disciples out of believers.

Dr. Jay Zinn, Founder of The Discipleship Group

There are few authors who can take theology and turn it into a devotional series of divine, inspiring nuggets of poetry. Ken Birks is an author who penetrates your heart and soul to know God better.

David Fredrickson, Sr. Pastor (Retired), Evangel Christian Fellowship, Sacramento, CA

Most true followers of Christ would agree that we are witnessing a time when self-serving Christianity is reaping the whirlwind of disunity, confusion, and fruitlessness. It is past time to listen to the voice of reason merely. Instead, we must respond with renewed minds, hearts, and actions.

Reviews and References

Ken's devotional and poetry are like a voice in the wilderness calling God's beloved away from all that distracts to Him who is jealous for His bride. The reader who hears and responds will bring joy to God's heart and encouragement to others who have put their hand to the plow.

Edward Becker, Senior Pastor, Naches Valley Community Church, Yakima, WA; Vice President, Antioch World Missions

This work is filled with Biblical truths and spiritual revelation that flow from a heart passionate for the Savior and His precious Bride, the Church. The majestic flow from theme to theme contains powerful prophetic revelation as God calls His end-time warriors to arise. I was also amazed by each poem. The words were Davidic and musical, flowing like delightful streams with heavenly impartations.

Jim Feeney, Ph.D., Former Sr. Pastor, and Webmaster at Pentecostal Bible Studies and Free Pentecostal Sermon Central

I've known Pastor Ken Birks for several decades. He and I have worked in various ministerial capacities in the same family of churches. Ken is held in extremely high esteem among our many pastoral colleagues. He is a minister with a firm grasp of the Word of God, a wide variety of administrative skills, a heart for souls, a proven experiential familiarity with the gifts of the Holy Spirit, and an unwavering commitment to the work of the Lord.

Reviews and References

Doug Hartline, University of California, Director of Information, Technology, Retired

Ken's work herein ensures God's Word shines from a different angle in a way that helps us to look at it in a much deeper and often more profound way. It provides us with the unique ability to understand and appreciate God's Word in ways we may never have thought of before. We are suddenly confronted with beauty and clarity to our perceptions of our world and God's Kingdom. Let Ken's ability to paint with words reveal the treasures of the Word of God to you in colors you may never have perceived before.

Online Connections

www.kenbirks.com
Sowing Seeds of Faith, Bible Studies. Sermons, and More

www.straitarrow.net
Bible Studies, Sermons, Poetry, Devotionals, Podcasts, Seminars

www.straitarrow.net/devotional-poetry
Biblical Devotional Poetry

www.straitarrow.net/devotionals
Daily Devotionals

www.straitarrow.net/Newsletters
Bi-Monthly Newsletters

www.booksbyken.com
How to order Ken's books and materials

www.sacramento-wedding-officiants.com
Wedding Officiating

Email: klbirks@gmail.com

X Formerly Twitter: @klbirks

www.ingramcontent.com/pod-product-compliance
Lightning Source LLC
Chambersburg PA
CBHW061810070526
44586CB00024B/2795